Loves
IMPRESSIONS

Spiritual Poetry Collection

Kenneth Alexander

Balboa Press books may be ordered through booksellers or by contacting:

Balboa Press
A Division of Hay House
1663 Liberty Drive
Bloomington, IN 47403
www.balboapress.com
1 (877) 407-4847

Because of the dynamic nature of the Internet, any web addresses or links contained in this book may have changed since publication and may no longer be valid. The views expressed in this work are solely those of the author and do not necessarily reflect the views of the publisher, and the publisher hereby disclaims any responsibility for them.

Any people depicted in stock imagery provided by Thinkstock are models, and such images are being used for illustrative purposes only. Certain stock imagery © Thinkstock.

ISBN: 978-1-4525-1468-0 (sc)
ISBN: 978-1-4525-1469-7 (e)

Library of Congress Control Number: 2014908805

Printed in the United States of America.

Balboa Press rev. date: 09/12/2014

BALBOA
PRESS
A DIVISION OF HAY HOUSE

Dedicated to

Alexander Stevens, my grandfather, July 21, 1897 - August 12, 1976

To my children, Michael and Lauren Stevens,

To my parents Arthur and Marian Stevens.

Poetry by

Kenneth Alexander

SPIRITUAL POETRY COLLECTION

HEAVENS GATE

Leave earth behind and have heaven now

The past is the past…right here oh wow,

This place is beautiful…and …full of love,

I feel….different, kind of ….above,

Above what you might ask, …the past of earth,

The anger…the sadness..and greed from birth,

Too many poisons …for all the senses,

Earth tempted us ….to look through false lenses,

Illusion's ….we thought real,

Making A's , climbing ladders,….big job….big deal,

Striving and yearning to have or …have not,

The Smith's …the Jones'es and Societies lot,

Thank heaven for now,

Thank God today,

We can change ourselves instantly with forgiveness I say,

For once all is neutral and kindness prevails,

The path of truth…. will lift all our sails,

The ark of our knowledge will save us this time,

As we approach this new heaven… the past left behind,

Be in the now, ….enter heaven's gate,

Be kind …Be gentle,….Be loving …..Be great.

THE SUN SHINES IN ALL OF US

We live our unique lives

Waking happily by the light of the sun,

Our day if we choose…..can be light and much fun,

For many days the sun shines brightly from above,

We take for granted the sun's power and God's unconditional love,

Rays and beams of unending warm light,

How nice the heat feels, …oh what a delight,

For those of us who choose to stay hidden from it's powerful rays ,

Only feel powerless and know of only dark and cold days,

Everyone…I mean everyone…. knows the sun shines each day,

Even blind people know this…. And they make their own way,

They shine brightly and use the gifts that they have got,

Never once looking at the sun did the blind man say that is my blind spot,

For what we cannot see in darkness……

Does not mean there isn't light,

You see the sun shines always…always somewhere,….. day or night,

So be like the sun, and shine bright for all your days,

When clouds lurk amongst you in life and block the sun's rays,

You, …. You be the light and shine your unique way,

Because the sun shines in all of us… each moment of each day.

LOVE

Love is an endless flow and glorious seed,

It is eternal, it is powerful, it is kind indeed,

Love is a river of wealth from the heart,

To love yourself first, to be kind, to be real,

To accept all your wrinkles, dimples and appeal,

For one can learn first from this act of love,

Now love God and fellow man, be like above,

Let your love fly, let is soar, let it cover the earth,

Love is a state of being that knows no compare,

To be giving , forgiving, and accepting with care,

As love grows stronger and stronger with constant use,

We embrace life through love and shed all abuse,

For living in love and loving life complete and whole,

Is a balance we seek to nourish our soul,

For each second, minute and hour of each day,

Matter not if love is not present I say,

Time is not relevant if love cannot prosper,

True wealth in life is the love we encounter,

Take each moment as a gift of love,

God sprinkles kisses, hugs, and warmth from above,

To strengthen and remind us how love is the way,

Show love in each second,

minute and hour of each day.

DIVINE CONNECTION
U + GOD = Happy Face

As above, so below,

A river of energy does now flow,

For divine light shining from high above,

Flows through my brain, my body, my heart of love,

For mother earth returns the favor,

By sending energy upward to savor,

The pulse of lava from earths core,

Up through your feet, your knees and more,

As energies mix and combine in the heart,

This day is sacred and ready to start,

Go forth with courage and confidence and glee,

You shine and brighten life for all to see,

You are showing up, you are unique and new,

Leading the way, responsibly connected through and through.

THERE IS ALWAYS TIME FOR LOVE

There is always time for love

Each moment is precious and uniquely ours,

We can do better by seeing it is really God's,

For what a moment is for sure it is a vote of grace,

A time God grants us and the whole human race,

To not compare one lovely second to the next,

But to realize our creative power in it to manifest,

Not what we selfishly might think,

But real love for others

reaching out without a blink,

For this time of the moment is granted by God's love,

It is heaven sent, it is joyous, it is from above,

To say there is not enough time is not true,

To say you have not loved enough in it might clear your view,

For when you love all in each moment

it becomes clear,

That there is infinite time to love others,

as God is love, as time appears.

GOD'S LOVE

God's love flows like waters breathe,

Like airs presence, like a bakeries scent,

This divine love is always there,

You can enjoy, and have it if you care,

Care to honor God's creation in you,

Loving yourself first through and through,

Loving others is step two… my brothers,

Creating love for yourself and for others,

Now you are peaceful , happy and still,

In the stillness, is strength and power of will,

Will I honor God now and forever,

Will I seek love in every person place and thing,

For this action of loving one another,

Opens access to God's love for every sister and brother,

For creations of love know no equal,

When you love in and love out,

There is only love as a sequel,

Love of another is God's love in disguise,

For God is in all man no matter the size.

LOVE ANEW.......THROUGH AND THROUGH

It is said that love is blind, but that is not true,

Love is certainly kind,

Love is pure......... love is fresh and new,

This does not happen by cherishing your love,

It only happens by staying present and peaceful like a dove,

For holding on to love from days gone by,

Is merely thwarting your full love now…so try,

Let those old times of love be cast aside,

Let your full love flourish and not hide,

For love is not a part time job,

Love is full time, 100% , and beaming inside,

For loving completely and all in,

Does not allow for another heart or you to win,

For pining secretly for past desire,

For spirit and love that no one can admire,

Love is open , love is clean, and love is bold,

Love is real, love is caring , love is not cold,

Sometimes to be real and honest,

We must cut our ties and leave our love life's forest,

For comfort zones are only illusions,

And staying in the woods of love, loses sight of conclusions,

For finishing strong and loving yourself true,

requires bold action, integrity, and a clean field of view,

New purpose , new joy, new love you seek,

You deserve the best, your love is real, you are blessed not meek.

Love calls you to a new place

and love is waiting for you there too,   So love anew ...through and through.

LOVE

Love is neither right or wrong,

Love is amazing when it takes shape in a song,

For love is ever present in the air we breathe,

We are selective in what we inhale from when we teethe,

For inhaling the air of anger , hate ,blame or sadness,

is a waste of God's precious creation ,your lungs…and short of madness,

for inhaling joy and peace and love,

Is what was granted and graced and sanctioned from above,

But going it alone, making up your own mind, letting your ego decide,

Erased God out from the love you may wish to hide,

Be grateful for the love of God and see what possibly in your mind is slanted,

Your perception may be off a bit….less than enchanted,

Declare a new space, a new eternity in this second we call life,

Inhale love, hold it in , then exhale hate and anger and strife,

Hold your breath now before you inhale,

Let gratitude be on your mind for the love that is near,

For as you breathe anew and hold love in your heart dear,

Your lungs will be smiling and loving your heart clear,

with loving oxygen that clears the air of all cares and concerns,

Congratulations my friend, your breathing love now …. your heart yearns,

To forgive your mind and let it all go,

For truth be told ..the heart leads with love and the brain is in tow,

Inhale, exhale, only love in and out,

When love finds you smiling it is because you brought love all about.

MY LOVE

My love for you

Is special and unique

It is a kind of love

The kind you seek

For love is not about the doing with others

Love is about just being….with each other

Being is….a quiet space

Being is …..a time for grace

Being is…..such that less can be more

Being is still, yet still means more

More time to hear the silence of our love

More time to connect with the oneness from above

For as one we are abundantly smart

To share and care together as one heart

I love you,

Dad

THE FALCON'S LOVE

As I stood beneath the Falcon in a tree,

It stood stoic and tall and quiet as could be,

In the Falcon I gazed into the eyes of heaven above,

The Falcon felt welcome,   the Falcon felt my love,

I asked for Gods healing and the Falcon complied,

He looked directly at me and he never sighed,

Truth, and wisdom were present this day,

I felt all his knowledge and wisdom and say,

The Falcon is love, the Falcon is God, the Falcon is forever one with me,

As I gave thanks and bid my farewell, but what did I see,

his mate proudly perched on the other side of the tree.

With love and compassion I connected with her,

She healed me further and now I healed her,

God works through all of us especially today,

The Falcons who were in a tree showed me the way.

A MOTHER'S LOVE

From that instant in time where an egg is made mortal,

A mother's love commences as if through a portal,

A Journey of bliss and joyful pains and pleasures,

Feeling a new heartbeat, a kick, or a tussle for good measure,

A baby grows and with God's grace is born anew,

Given life on earth and a gift for a new mother too,

To feed a child from a breast so plump,

To nurture and caress the newborn,

mother now gone with the baby bump,

Crawling on all fours is a treasure,

A distant memory when that first step is taken

and …that's ours to pleasure,

For reliving our independence through our

child's eyes and right to walk freely,

Is only for an instant when a mothers "no" is heard

….constantly, both daily and weekly,

For being a mom is a 24/7 affair,

Bathing, cleaning up and combing the hair,

All A's seems like a personal win,

When a child pleases you with your desired hopes with a grin,

When they bring home a grade less than d,

You console as if it is not the world's worst thing that could ever be,

For a mother's love looks out from beginning to end,

Unconditionally her love is and always will be that of a friend,

To know her and love her is her just reward,

God knows she carried and picked up blocks or dolls until she got tired
and then snored,

A mother's love goes beyond and above,

Unseen is the prayer and appeal to keep you safe and given God's love,

For a Mothers love is holy and divine as it should be,

Creating new life is the greatest complement a mother grants others
and God to see,

That one day this "wee" toddler becomes a beautiful girl or a "gent",

From a single cell, an incredible creation called life is heaven sent,

A Mother's love is complete when her child gives new life too,

Becoming a grandma is validation that her child has now grew,

Grew to know that life is precious and that it is the worth time and sweat,

To be humble and to love, till Gods breath is met,

A Mother's love is redeeming as a life of joy and God's pleasing,

To know that her child is happy and well until the day she stops breathing.

For a Mothers love is eternal, she works through and through,

Insuring that every day is a good day for her child

… there is nothing she is not willing to do.

Thank you Mom for everything you did for me

Love, Kenny

MY GRANDPA'S LOVE

My grandpa lived in Florida when I was just a boy,

His mobile home was his place and he loved it like joy,

He would come visit during summers when the weather was hot,

His white Buick Skylark… was the car that traveled far from his lot,

It was his love for his grandkids and golf that fueled his desire to par,

Par not the golf course, but to par his life and be our north star,

Although birdie is better and eagle is one better than that,

Grandpa was not into showing off although he did sport a straw hat,

He did get a hole in one, an ashtray for a prize,

I have yet to get a hole in one, but it would be a great surprise,

The times that we shared were special indeed,

He loved our dog ruff and picnicking gave all of us shade tree,

I loved to be with him and he showed me how to golf,

By hitting golf balls in a field, every shot was a boost to my own self,

For there was not a target and there was no judgment,

Just hit it out there and then hit it back… it was a special moment,

Where nothing was said, no instruction or way to progress,

My grandpa knew what was most important,

It was not about distance, direction or speed,

You see he knew only that sharing time with us was all that we need,

I love my grandpa for he was always a friend,

He was gentle and kind and kept us safe in the end,

It was hard when he left as I did not get to say goodbye,

Even now as I write this … it brings tears and I cry,

That everyone who reads this will love their grandpa more,

Hug them and squeeze them, go on errands with them, go to the store,

Find ways to love your grandpa and write them or just share your view,

For Grandpa's are special and they deserve to be cared for too,

Thank you Alexander Stevens for sharing your days,

sharing your name with me as my middle name

I see now a new way,

that you are always with me, ….. it was hidden from my view,

I need not say goodbye because your always with me ….. how true.

Eternally grateful, Ken

A sincere "Thank You" to God for inspiring me to write these
poems in God's timing and in God's expanse.

KENNETH ALEXANDER

Kenneth Alexander Stevens was born in Elmhurst, Queens New York in 1960. He dedicates this book of poems to his grandfather Alexander Stevens thus the reason the poetry pen name, Kenneth Alexander. He resides in Orlando, Florida. He has 2 children, Michael and Lauren Stevens, pictured in the "My Love" poem.

Ken is a keynote speaker on Creativity, Performance Coach, and Creator. His mission in life is to help others to reach for their peak potential, and have fun doing it while being appreciative of all life.

He has 11 US Patents and has developed many products that have given joy to many. He is called higher to "show up" and help raise the human potential in every human being through his creativity training and awareness information products.

My Ten Core Values for life and business success

I FREELY CHOOSE TO:

Love All: Even when it is my greatest challenge.

Respect Life: Even the smallest creature when possible.

Honor: The greatness within each person, known and potential.

Share: Gods time with others.

Create: Be conscious of every moment and each creation in it.

Be Truthful: Let every moment be so.

Enjoy : myself, my family, my friends, and all I connect to.

Be Gracious: We are human born to reach, possibly fail and willing to forgive.

Be Humble: Live in the world not of the world.

Succeed: Each moment is precious. Make life fun and profitable

Look for future poetic writings from Kenneth Alexander

RESPECT LIFE COLLECTION

HONOR COLLECTION

SHARE COLLECTION

CREATE COLLECTION

TRUTH COLLECTION

JOY COLLECTION

GRACE COLLECTION

HUMILITY COLLECTION

LIVE COLLECTION

Sample Poems from future

REVELATIONS

Spiritual Poetry Collections

Kenneth Alexander

Faith

Faith is a knowing that knows no bounds,

It is complete, whole, assured as easy as that sounds,

For faith has no eyes no ears, or touch,

Faith just is if that is too much,

Too much for you to handle, my simplicity revealed,

When I am at your core, in your door, in your mind it is sealed,

Sealed with certainty that you will prevail,

Oceans upon oceans a child can sail,

For truly faith is symbolically upon trust,

Three God's in one, remember all of us,

As you pray your simple prayer, hear your heart keep us truly there,

The faith will be present, all will be well without further care.

Journey home

Many times in my life we journey home,

As if this one place is the only place we roam,

For it has a past, it feels good, moms cooking to taste,

The memories of pies and meals, the look on her face,

To see the truth you realize now she was your home too,

Your nine month home, a womb to love, your mom alive with you,

That first home indeed, a place to grow, a seed unleashed too,

The look of your dad, when mom spring news,

a new home now there is two,

Two precious likes, two in covenant, two as one a home,

A journey ensued as you did grow and then you would dome,

You won all around, a sight to see, a home ready to leave too,

Your born into love and brought to see a new home for you,

Thank God you made it … your loving heart joined to a new start won,

Born today with God we pray …your blessed in your new home to have fun.

Witness

In life we observe many days and memories,

The witness we are can be amazing in many ways,

What then do we see when we observe a tragedy,

We look through a lens and allow judgment to be,

A way it was, our view of it all, oh what a shame,

There must be a reason, someone's at fault, find someone to blame,

Through God's lens it is different, impartial and free,

A look through the lens of love will help you to see,

The good are great in every way shape and form,

To see performance of responders to see compassion and warm,

Warm your heart to the love that exists side by side,

In all things there is love, you can now go wide,

Wide with your viewpoint, ease up, see the truth,

Each moment there is love, be a witness and sooth,

That time to remember when you observed other people doing right,

Witnessing the God within, the God in all, the love that is in plain sight.

Worth

Life is so precious to and that adhere,

To the simplicity of kindness and love that appear,

Human nature, a way of being, people peaceful and warm,

A loving touch, a reassuring word, listening till dawn,

To value a life is it worth contemplating it,

There is no yardstick or tape measure with love stamped to fit,

The everlasting, eternal grandeur of God's gift to all,

Please hold all your questions… it's not your call,

For a life's worth is an ongoing expanse,

Long after your physical presence, there is still a dance,

For your creative expressions live on forever more,

Timeless treasures made here… creations to adore,

So live your life knowing that your worth is always on the rise,

Whether your tall or short or any particular size,

For it only matters that you breathe in and out too,

It is worth it my friend to rejoice, and say thank you to God for the precious you.

Angels

The angels sing and dance with joy it really is a party,

For Angels have assignments… to carry out God's Mardi,

A Mardi Gras, a vast parade a celebration of the day,

The day you came to earth a man, naked baby way,

Complete, whole, and open to all …the love of many,

Many others that before you came the same way very,

Very happy, very loved, very glad, very peaceful too,

These Angels that received love first they paved the way for you,

To carry peace and love forward now, …nothing more a need,

To release all ill or misconception of God's plead,

To stay the course, straight toward love joy and peace,

This may be simple, Angel's sigh, please pay attention to these,

These elementary Angel's rules, guidelines to divine will,

For each and every one of you are Angels in the flesh to fill,

My beautiful harvest, the mass of humanity, growing ripe for me,

Let Angels be, let them love and serve, God bless them all happily.

Choice

What is a choice in life? It really is fun,

To look at each day and decision, what about this one?,

I choose this, I choose that, you are decisive indeed,

The choice of not choosing, a choice to seed,

Seed another day to make that choice, can't face it now,

What's wrong you're looking at it, go ahead allow,

Allow you to accept wherever you are,

Be your own best friend, pat your back, love yourself …you're a star,

A bright star at that, with a lamp shade on it,

The lamp shade of indecision… you will soon quit,

Covering up your beauty, your brilliant light,

Make the choice, the tough one, it will all work out,

You can ease all the struggle with God at the helm,

Allow your choice with his guidance, it's a new realm,

To boldly go forth caring to be your best yet … lose the shade don't fret,

The choice is made, glad you stayed, making a choice it is now set.

Value

What I value the most in each human being,

Is the spirit that is built over each and every season,

Life is a rhythm of seeding and harvest,

It is likely that value is what separates the best,

For valuing life and each moment of creation,

Is a human spirit's soul work and vocation,

To create anew… every day looking forward once more,

Never turning around, going forth, ready to soar,

Soar higher still as spirit gains value and grace,

Realizing other spirits matter… it is not a race,

For valuing others work and appreciating their role,

In life this is God's plan and no bell to toll,

Ring true as you are… value your inner gift,

God loves your value, your spirit, you rise… he will lift.

Excited

It is a great feeling to go through life with faith in,

To see all as a blessing, even when things look dim,

For the hope of better in your mind keeps the spirit up,

With a sense gratitude, thank you for all, even my pup,

I am excited now, good things can begin to show the world a man,

That endured a lot in life, mostly his own plan,

To keep him from his greatness, to keep him from his day,

This is not without trying, he did everything his way,

He created it all, now he owned it, that is a big step agree,

When you are responsible to your life, your responsible to God in thee,

Get excited you are the one, who took action to arrive,

Going forward to a new destination, this is how we thrive,

By pushing forth, sharing it all, giving every ounce,

Let God flow through your being, …your message to be announced.

The Art

Showing up in life is quite the art,

There are so many facets and choices when to start,

Start from where you be, center yourself in me,

For the guiding light of truth and freedom too,

Is at hand and flows through you to be,

A child of God most holy and revered,

One so mighty, bold, and confident you stared,

Straight towards fear and busted through its illusion,

Took on the world, made a stand, their concluding,

You know the art, you know it well,

You are God's centerpiece for her to tell,

Others Angels and Saints, a creator's blog,

For the art of showing up is not for me to gloat,

It is an act of kindness, love and peace for ones self to note.

Love

Love is a very strong emotional muscle,

When we love so much it can feel like a rustle,

A rustle of joy as we go about our loving way,

Seeing the best in others, enjoying every day,

For this heaven we are creating is our peaceful place,

It really is quite impressive to get healed with much grace,

For forgiving yourself completely is loving yourself true,

Loving yourself whole and complete, step one for you,

Thank you for this love of yourself, rinse and repeat be sure,

You can always love yourself, enough, that is good before,

Before loving others and pouring God's love through you,

Respect yourself and mind your health the answer is in view,

To begin all you can be for yourself and others too,

Be the giving person that God has birthed a new,

Let your love and your spirit bless others and shine through.

Available Heart

I love myself whole, my heart available to thee,

I have cleansed my past, my heart available and free,

Free to be true to the world and myself,

To create love openly, not stored on a shelf,

For building romance is not by loose talk,

It is by making friends, being kind, a beach to walk,

To share human thoughts and emotions and release,

For to love again one must cease,

Cease all strings of meaningless barter and banter,

Creating true love is pure not with any cancer,

For cancer holds on with a grip to hurt,

But pure love is open, nourishing without flirt,

Pure love is what I intend to create,

My available heart is open to the world and the feeling is great.

Printed in the United States
By Bookmasters